# FREDERIK VII
## The Giver of
## the Constitution

by Jens Gunni Busck

## Historika

Published in cooperation with the Royal Danish Collection

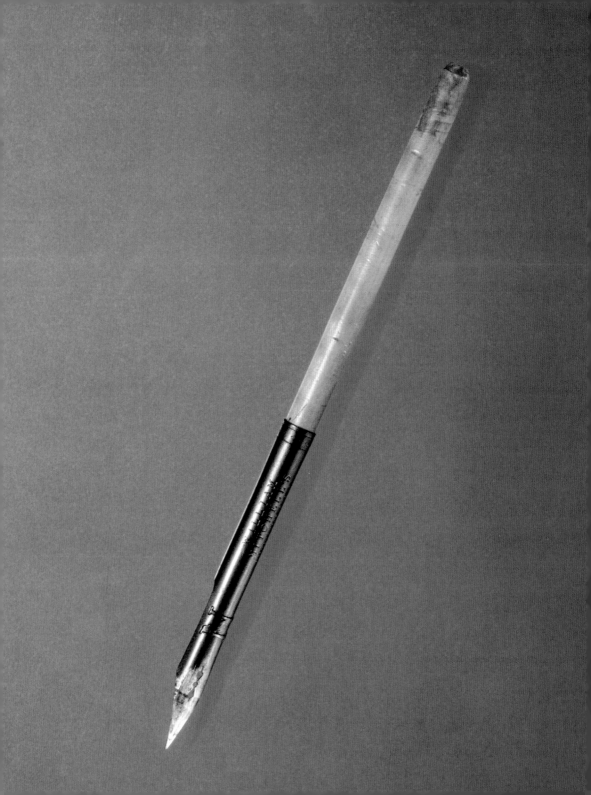

# CONTENTS

With this humble pen, Frederik VII signed the Constitution of the Kingdom of Denmark on 5 June 1849.

# THE POPULAR SCANDAL-MAKER

**Frederik VII spent the first forty years of his life demonstrating that he neither wished to nor could take on the responsibility of governing as an absolute monarch. He was an incorrigible liar who ruined his marriages, drank too much, and mixed with the common people in a way that was unheard-of for a successor to the throne. Nevertheless, he ended up being regarded as one of the great names among the Danish monarchs, and this was because he possessed an ability to perceive his limitations, which is rare among kings. Frederik VII gave up from the beginning, and precisely for this reason, he was able to ensure that he would be surprisingly regarded positively by posterity.**

Frederik VII playing chess with Countess Danner.

Danes have heard about the time when the people's representatives approached the king and asked him to transfer political power to them, which the king thought was a good idea. Representative democracy was thus peacefully introduced in Denmark, in contrast to the course of events in many other places, and people like to suggest that the episode constitutes evidence of a peculiar Danish tendency to solve problems in a civilized fashion. This is a story of which one is reminded on squares and in public places throughout the country where there are busts and statues of the giver of the constitution.

Frederik VII's remarkable fate was to become a popular icon who stood for representative democracy, and he made the monarchy popular in a way it had never been before. His love for the people was as genuine as it was sentimental, and his motto, "The love of the people—my strength," signalled the advent of a new age in which the monarch became a symbol of national unity. The civil war that took place during the years 1848-1850 accompanied the implementation of the constitution and played an important role in making Frederik VII the people's king. The war forged national solidarity that for many Danes made representative democracy and love of the fatherland two aspects of the same thing. The war did not produce any result at all, but it made the king extremely popular among the populace.

The King needed all the support he could get, for Frederik VII lived his whole life in opposition to the world from which he came. His tall tales, his wild living, and his childlessness were the cause of endless annoyance at Amalienborg, and things got no better after his accession to the throne. With two wrecked arranged marriages behind him, the king married Louise Rasmussen, who had been born a commoner and whom the king ennobled as the Countess of Danner. This was widely condemned as a violation of the social order and provoked strong reactions both within Denmark and elsewhere. The scandal isolated the king politically and socially but did not reduce his popularity among the common people, and they therefore became his most important allies.

In general, Denmark's first constitutional monarch was a man of contradictions. He made himself a man of the people, but he remained high above the people. He was antiauthoritarian despite the fact that he was an authority figure himself. And though he had not wished for power, his actions had a decisive effect on Danish history on a number of occasions.

## Fritz and his parents

Prince Frederik Carl Christian was born on 6 October 1808; the prince's parents were Prince Christian (VIII) Frederik (1786–1848) and his cousin, Princess Charlotte Frederikke of Mecklenburg-Schwerin (1784–1840). The prince's father was the cousin of Frederik VI and the obvious candidate to accede to the Danish throne, as the King had neither sons nor brothers. It was therefore highly likely that the newborn would be next after his father, so Christian Frederik was offended when no cannon salutes were fired to mark the occasion of the birth. Salutes were fired the following day because he had complained to the King.

Fritz, as the prince was called, was the product of a marriage in crisis. Christian Frederik was a gifted young man of whom there were great expectations, and the family had not approved of his marriage to Charlotte Frederikke. With her

Frederik VII's mother, Princess Charlotte Frederikke, holding an embroidery frame. While she was living in exile in Jutland, she had her son's measurements sent to her and sewed clothes for him. Unknown artist.

unstable temperament, she was poorly suited for life at the court, and Fritz was only a year old when his mother was banished from Copenhagen after having been discovered in an intimate situation with her singing instructor. Frederik VI did not like scandals, and the boy therefore never saw his mother again.

Charlotte Frederikke was first assigned a residence in Altona, but here, too, she caused so much trouble that she was instead parked in Horsens and forbidden

to travel farther than to Aarhus. However, Christian Frederik did keep her informed with regard to her son's progress, and a portrait of him was sent to her every year. When he was old enough, he and his mother began writing to each other directly, but—and this is indicative of the extent to which they were trusted—both the letters written by the prince's mother and those written by the prince himself were subject to being read by censors, even after the prince had become an adult.

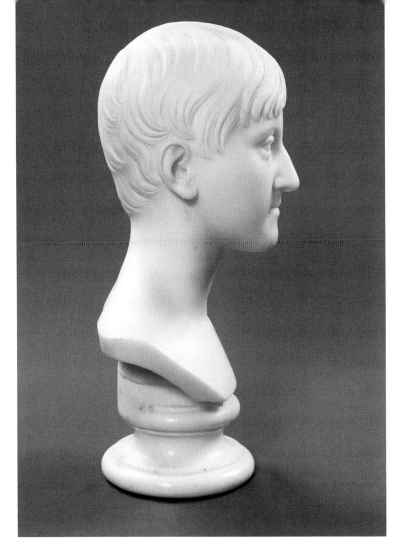

Frederik VII as a child, modelled by Bertel Thorvaldsen in 1820 and sculpted in marble in 1825. The world-famous sculptor again modelled a bust when Fritz was in Rome in 1828 and subsequently praised the prince for not pretending to be a greater person than he was.

After the banishment of Charlotte Frederikke, Fritz was first in the custody of the queen, but during the first eight years of his life, he was particularly attached to his nanny, Christiane Reiersen. Fritz resided primarily in his parents' palace at Amalienborg and spent long periods with his paternal aunt, Princess Juliane, at Sorgenfri Palace. Another important figure for the young prince was his governor and teacher J. F. Bardenfleth, who taught Fritz together with his own son, Carl Emil Bardenfleth, who was about the prince's age and would also make his mark on Danish history in 1848.

Frederik VII – The Giver of the Constitution

Fritz developed an early interest in antiquities that is believed to have been encouraged by his nanny, who read a great deal. This became a lifelong passion for Fritz, and he eventually launched and participated in a long series of archaeological excavations. The burial mound was drawn by the world-famous German painter Caspar David Friedrich when Friedrich was attending the Royal Danish Academy of Fine Arts in Copenhagen in the late 1790s, at the same time as Christian Frederik.

Frederik VI with Queen Marie and their daughters, Vilhelmine and Caroline, painted by C. W. Eckersberg in 1821. Of the couple's eight children, only these two princesses had survived. The king was interested in getting one of them married to one of his potential successors, doubtless in order to secure the viability of his own branch of the House of Oldenburg in the line of succession to the Danish throne.

During the years 1813 and 1814, Christian Frederik was the governor and briefly the constitutional king of Norway, but he returned home when Sweden forced him to give up the Norwegian crown. Frederik VI was very dissatisfied with the constitution his cousin had introduced in Norway against his will, and to punish Christian Frederik, the King created a superfluous post for him as governor of Funen. Fritz therefore ended up living at Odense Palace with his father and his father's new wife, Princess Caroline Amalie of Augustenburg, who was now to take on the role of the prince's mother; the prince's beloved nanny was fired. In 1818, Fritz accompanied his parents on a tour of Germany, but he had to stay home when Christian Frederik and Caroline Amalie undertook a three-year journey abroad starting the following year. The prince's father produced an extremely detailed plan for the raising of his son during his absence in which he describes Fritz as good-natured and talented, but warns of his tendency not to be truthful.

During the summer of 1821, the prince had an accident involving a gun that exploded. This cost him a piece of his left thumb, and he later claimed that the injury was the result of a war wound. Around this time, Fritz generally began to develop in a problematic direction, and it was reported to his father that Fritz had chronic difficulties concentrating. When the prince turned thirteen that same year, he was made a colonel by Frederik VI, but after the king had attended an examination in which the prince had participated the following year, Frederik VI had to declare that he was disappointed by the boy's development.

## The grand tour

Disappointment over the prince's development did not prevent the king from engineering the engagement of Fritz and the king's youngest daughter, Princess Vilhelmine. There was a particular reason for this: Ever since Frederik VI and his circle had forced Hereditary Prince Frederik (Christian Frederik's official father) to hand over power to them, there had been a tense relationship between the two branches of the royal family. The King had first wished to arrange a marriage between Christian Frederik and his eldest daughter, Princess Caroline, but this was rendered impossible by Christian Frederik's marriage to Charlotte Frederikke, and as Frederik VI no longer had hopes of producing a crown prince

himself, it was dynastically meaningful to arrange a marriage between Fritz and Vilhelmine. There would hardly have been any concerns about inbreeding, as it was probably known to all—but unmentionable!—that Christian Frederik was not the biological son of the hereditary prince and that Fritz therefore did not, strictly speaking, belong to the Oldenburg line of kings.

The engagement was announced in 1826, but the family was very concerned about the prince's immaturity. It was therefore decided that Fritz would be sent to Switzerland for a lengthy stay in the company of two trusted companions, who were granted authority to act in loco parentis. Once again, Christian Frederik dictated a strict program for his son, whose education was to continue while he was abroad. Fritz would be away from Denmark for two years, and the prince later described his experiences as his life's greatest pleasures.

From the beginning, the stay in Switzerland went well, though the prince sometimes indulged his urges to tell tall tales, as when, at an inn, he told the local priest that he had once shot a disobedient servant. Fritz had a special ability to get people on his wavelength, and he soon became popular in Geneva. The prince was an excellent marksman and won a number of prizes in the local shooting societies. He also enrolled as a private in the city's National Guard unit and participated in social life, which meant that his companions had to keep a close eye on him. It was problematic that in conversation with other guests, he claimed that he had secretly converted to Catholicism, and because of his inappropriate interest in a young British widow, it became necessary to drag Fritz off on a long tour of the south of France.

After having spent almost a year and a half in Switzerland, Fritz travelled on to Italy, where he had an audience with the Pope (but did not claim to be a Catholic on that occasion!) and enjoyed himself together with representatives of the Scandinavian artists' colony in Rome. During a subsequent stay in Naples, the prince once again had a brief dalliance with a woman that caused his guardians to become concerned, but the object of his attentions suddenly left the city. No one knows why.

The prince travelled north during the summer of 1828, and after another stay in Switzerland, the company reached Denmark a few days before the wedding, which took place on November 1. In Schleswig, Fritz had met with Christian Frederik and Duke Friedrich Wilhelm of Glücksburg-Sonderburg-Beck, who had coordinated parts of the journey. The duke had kept himself informed with regard to the prince's behaviour and considered it necessary to forbid his own sons—including the future Christian IX—to associate with Fritz. His comment in this connection was "That fellow isn't worth a charge of powder."

## Princess Vilhelmine

Despite the fact that the state coffers were depleted and Frederik VI was parsimonious, no expense was spared in connection with the wedding. The celebra-

Princess Vilhelmine, painted by Louis Aumont in 1831. In 1838, following her disastrous marriage to Fritz, Vilhelmine married her cousin, Duke Carl, who was an older brother of the future Christian IX and participated in the First Schleswig War on the Schleswig-Holstein side.

Within the royal family, Fritz had a kind of counterpart in his uncle, Prince (later Hereditary Prince) Ferdinand, who was Christian Frederik's younger brother. Like Fritz, Ferdinand cared little for the stiff etiquette of life at court but liked gambling and the company of women. The year after Fritz's marriage to Vilhelmine, the two branches of the royal family were further linked by an arranged marriage between Ferdinand and Frederik VI's eldest daughter, Princess Caroline.

tion was a demonstration of power that was intended to secure the new order of succession and show that the Oldenburg royal line had splendid prospects for the future. On the eve of the wedding, Copenhagen was illuminated by lights in all windows, and the festivities continued for the better part of a week. The wedding was also celebrated in the market towns of the kingdom, for example in Horsens, where there was a parade and salutes were fired at Charlotte Frederikke's palace. The prince's mother remained unwelcome in the capital, but after the wedding, she was finally allowed to leave Horsens and moved to Rome, where she remained until her death.

The newlyweds were installed in the newly refurbished Brockdorff's Palace (now Frederik VIII's Palace) at Amalienborg; their parents resided in the two palaces next door. Fritz now had to live with constantly being watched by his suspicious family. He continued his officer training, but his main task consisted of behaving well and awaiting the day he would become King. For Fritz, this was a suffocating situation, and his need for freedom expressed itself in frequent evenings of drinking in the city, after which he treated his well-behaved wife inconsiderately. There were frequent scenes in the couple's home in which the blind-drunk prince behaved threateningly, frightening the princess out of her wits, and Vilhelmine gradually came to spend much of her time in her parents' residence in the palace next door.

Fritz was unable to amuse himself when he was alone, and for this reason, he went out to eating and drinking establishments in the city as often as possible, and here, he made some important acquaintances. He found the ideal drinking partner in Carl Berling, who was a little younger than the prince and was the heir to the Berling publishing house. The prince also found himself a mistress named Jensine Weiner, with whom he was associated for a number of years. She was one of the members of the corps de ballet from the theatre who were invited to the exclusive nocturnal gatherings for the thirsty elite. Carl Berling, too, acquired a girlfriend from the corps de ballet; her name was Louise Rasmussen, and Fritz was also attracted to her. He later claimed that he had first met her when he was thirteen years old and she was half that age. Fritz, Berling, and Louise formed a clique of three that became an anchor of decisive importance to the prince. The two friends gave him the support and understanding he did not find in his family.

In 1832, Fritz got a welcome break from life at Amalienborg when he was sent to sea to take a summer tour around the Kattegat and the Baltic. This suited him excellently, and the following year, he was given command of a schooner on which he sailed to Bornholm for a visit of some length. However, the following winter, the winter of 1833–1834, was trying both for the prince and those around him. Back at his hated home at Amalienborg, he drank heavily in his own company while everyone at court turned against him. His coarseness toward his wife became worse and worse, and at a ball held by the Russian envoy, he insulted her in the presence of others. This was, of course, unacceptable, and when he came home drunk a few weeks later and threatened to kill her, it was the last straw for her father. Frederik VI visited Fritz at home and formally demanded that he hand over his sabre and move to Jægerspris Palace.

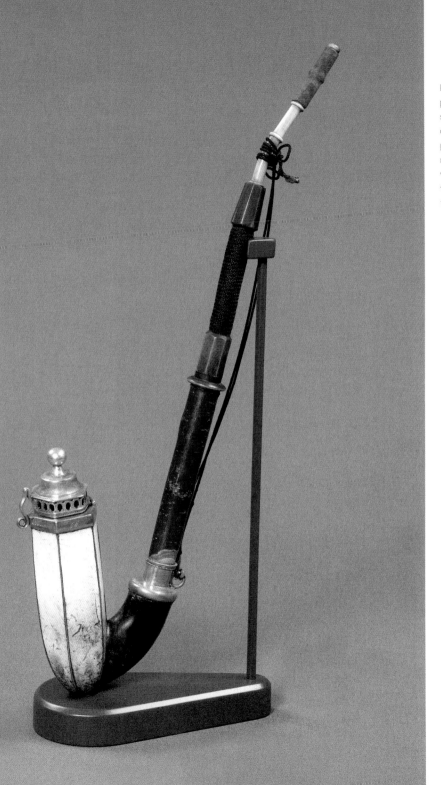

Fritz was a passionate pipe smoker from an early age. The picture shows a meerschaum pipe with silver fittings that shows signs of frequent use.

Fritz was probably given this writing set in gilded bronze from the King of Prussia when he, Fritz, was a young man. Aside from correspondence, the prince liked to write short essays on antiquities and other subjects, and he also liked to draw, though he was only moderately talented.

## Banished from Copenhagen

"Actually, I do not know why we were separated," Fritz later said of his banishment in March 1834. In a way, one can understand him, for his transgressions were by no means as serious as those of predecessors such as Frederik V or Christian VII. Men in arranged marriages could demand certain freedoms, and Frederik VI and Christian Frederik also had mistresses, but they were discreet and let their wives retain their dignity as individuals who were officially ignorant of any infidelity. In contrast, Fritz had failed to maintain a respectable facade, and it was not insignificant that he was married to the King's favourite daughter.

The prince did not necessarily experience his confinement at Jægerspris as punishment. He was kept under observation and was not permitted to leave the palace unguarded, but he had finally been released from an environment he could not stand. He lost interest in alcohol—at least for a while—as soon as he was out of Copenhagen, and he was happy to learn that he would be allowed to carry out archaeological excavations in the Hornsherred giant tumulus. After a few weeks at Jægerspris, Fritz wrote to Frederik VI that he would like to be divorced from Vilhelmine, and this suited the King.

To keep his son constructively occupied and at an appropriate distance, Christian Frederik hurriedly arranged a scientific expedition to Iceland. It set forth in early May 1834, and Fritz is said to have been very enthusiastic about the high seas during the crossing. He spent a splendid summer in Iceland studying the country's antiquities and nature and confusing the inhabitants by riding around with his retinue on a little Icelandic horse wearing simple clothing.

After his banishment, Fritz was not welcome in the capital, but he himself had come up with the idea that the journey to Iceland could be followed by a stay in Fredericia during which he would have a military post. He was therefore appointed commander of the Funen Infantry Regiment, which was an empty title, as the regiment's unchallenged leader was the ageing fortress commandant and general F. J. C. Castonier. It was now the general's responsibility to keep the prince under control, but in reality, Fritz had more freedom than ever before. He did not have permission to travel to Zealand or leave Denmark, but to the extent this was allowed by his military duties, he was free to travel around Jutland and Funen. He continued to see Jensine Weiner, who moved with him to Fredericia, where, to his annoyance, she got married a few years later. He was also visited by Carl Berling and Louise, and while General Castonier had his female friend expelled from the town—having judged her to be another young woman of loose morals—he could not stop Fritz from continuing to correspond with her.

In Fredericia, Fritz laid the foundation of his image as the people's king. There are many stories of how he travelled around the area in poor clothing and visited farmers and other commoners. At the same time, the prince's little court gave new life to the town, and naturally, the local citizenry were delighted to have living among them a successor to the throne who did not consider himself too fine to associate with them. Probably, the stay in Fredericia also contributed to establishing the prince's attitude toward the question of Schleswig and Holstein's relationship with Denmark, which would end up overshadowing all other matters during his reign. The conflict began smouldering in the 1830s, and at an early stage Frederik—in fact under the influence of a fairly strong sentimental tendency—was leaning toward a nationalist stance.

Christian VIII in a
general's uniform,
painted by Joseph
Court around
the time of his
accession to the
throne.

In 1838, the general died, and the aged Frederik VI was too weak to take any further interest in the unruly prince. Finally, the prince was no longer treated like a disobedient child, and in December 1839, Frederik VI died and Christian Frederik became Christian VIII. This meant that Fritz became Crown Prince and could once again show his face in Copenhagen, but instead his childhood residence, Odense Palace, became his base, as his father appointed him his successor as governor of Funen.

## Crown Prince in Odense

The post as governor did not involve any significant practical responsibilities, but as in Fredericia, Fritz became popular in the town. He also followed in his father's footsteps by joining the local freemasons' lodge, thus beginning a chapter of his life about which we naturally know very little. However, we do know that he eventually became very much involved in freemasonry and followed Christian VIII as Grand Master of the Danish Order of Freemasons upon his succession to the throne in 1848.

Crown Princess Caroline Mariane, painted by J. S. Otto in 1841.

*Next spread:*
Fritz and Princess Mariane's wedding procession through Copenhagen on 22 June 1841.

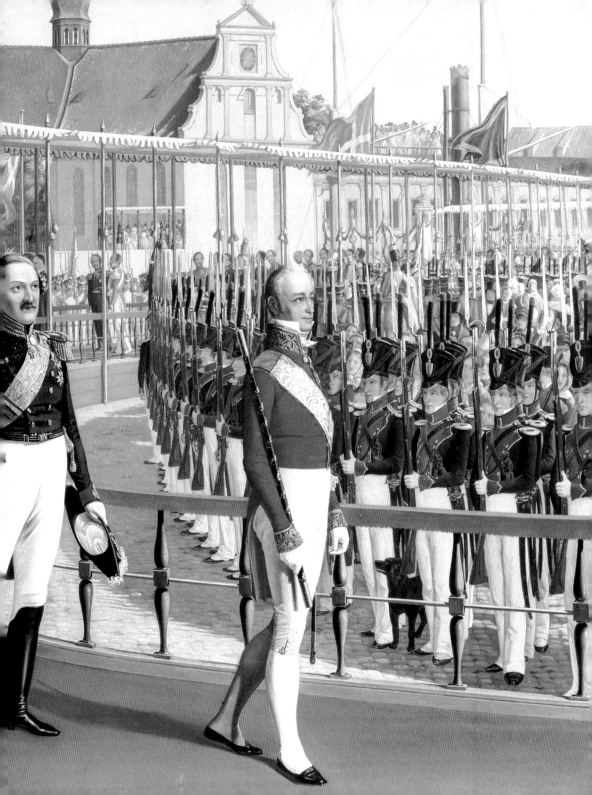

It was, of course, cause for concern that Fritz did not have an heir, so shortly after he became King, his father arranged for the prince to be engaged to the nineteen-year-old Duchess Caroline Mariane of Mecklenburg-Strelitz. Fritz acted the obedient son, and the pair were married in Germany on 10 June 1840, after which the marriage was celebrated in Copenhagen, though in a somewhat more subdued fashion than the prince's marriage in 1828. There was not much of a honeymoon, for during the months after the wedding, the prince was usually travelling without his wife. She later said that she had not been in Denmark a week when her inebriated husband introduced her to his "guardian angel," Louise Rasmussen. This was insulting, of course, but otherwise, Fritz did not behave maliciously as he had during his first marriage. Crown Princess Mariane he simply ignored, which could of course be just as bad, and like her predecessor, she sought consolation from her family. She regularly spent long periods in Germany, and in 1844, she had had enough and did not want to return to Denmark despite the fact that Fritz was sent down to Germany several times to convince her to return. Predictably enough, the marriage ended in a divorce two years later. Officially, Mariane was given the blame, but she was granted a generous pension by the Danish state.

Fritz preferred Louise, but she was still in a relationship with Carl Berling, who could not get his family's permission to marry her. The couple had a son in 1840 that had to be given up for adoption, and it has become known that in 1843, Fritz, too, became the father of a son. At least he took responsibility for paternity in a letter to the mother, Else Marie Poulsen, who appears to have been a servant girl at the court. It has widely been assumed that Fritz was unable to beget children due to a physical defect, but he himself appears not to have believed that this was the case.

Louise had to give up her position at the theatre because of a knee injury, and for some years, with the help of Berling, she ran a fashion business in Kongens Nytorv and then in Amagertorv. Her correspondence with Fritz during the 1840s indicates that the prince was deeply in love with her, and the FCL Company, as she called the clique consisting of Fritz, Carl, and Louise, had to withstand some emotional tensions. She and Berling were in the process of converting their relationship into a friendship while it began to appear possible that the retired ballerina could have a life together with Denmark's crown prince. Louise's visits to Fritz in Odense became longer, and during the period immediately prior to the prince's accession to the throne, she lived there almost permanently.

All his life, Fritz had sorrowed because he had been unable to see his banished mother, and there is no doubt that as the black sheep of the family, he felt that he shared his particular fate with Charlotte Frederikke. By getting himself banished, he had, in fact, followed in her footsteps, and he suffered a hard blow

Both during his childhood and when he was Crown Prince, Fritz's home was Odense Palace, in front of which, appropriately enough, there is now a full-figure statue of the King. He is holding out the Constitution with his right hand.

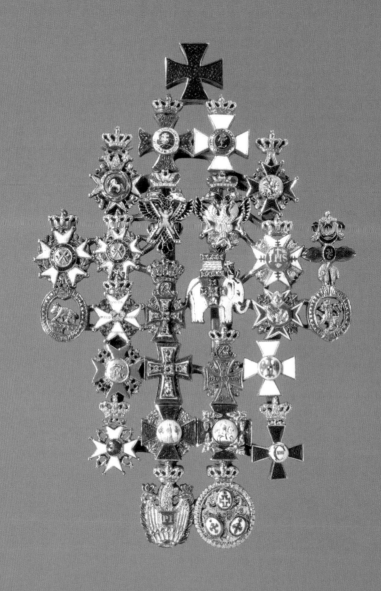

when his mother died in Rome in 1840 just when it finally would have been possible for him to see her. Now, however, Louise had decided to address his childhood trauma; she said, "He needs a mother, and I want to be a mother to him."

## The Fall of the Absolute Monarchy

Christian VIII had long known that the absolute monarchy's end was near. He wished to introduce a constitution as he had done in Norway, and Fritz had urged his father to carry out this plan so he would not have to take on the responsibility of governing. Implementation of Christian VIII's plan had thus far been prevented by the independence movement in Schleswig and Holstein that blossomed during the 1840s, but the work on a common constitution for the whole state (that is, the Kingdom plus the duchies) was well underway when the King suffered a lung infection shortly after New Year's Day 1848 and suddenly lay on his deathbed due to blood poisoning as a result of medical bloodletting. On his deathbed, he wrote a letter in which he asked his son to introduce the planned constitution and marry suitably before the end of the year.

Fritz had never been able to focus on his future role as King and dealt with the situation by drinking away his worries. Witnesses testified to how just a few days before his accession, the prince sat among drinking companions and referred to himself as Count Turd-kicker. But Christian VIII died on 20 January 1848, and Fritz took over the government immediately. A team of ministers were called together, and the new king also called in his politically inexperienced childhood friend, C. E. Bardenfleth, who had been the head of the prince's court in Odense and now became the King's closest advisor. On 28 January, to get the public, which was demanding reform, to grant the government some time, the government issued the so-called constitution rescript, which offered the prospect of a whole-state constitution that would give the Kingdom and the duchies common national assemblies with decision-making authority alongside the existing assemblies of the estates of the realm. The proclamation meant that the absolute monarchy would be abolished, and for a few weeks, it looked as though the transition from one system to another could be achieved without war.

Then the February revolution broke out in Paris. This sent shockwaves through Europe, and the duchies' representatives of the estates of the realm met in

When the absolute monarchy was abolished, the King insisted that he retain the sole right to grant titles and membership in royal orders, and he made use of this right frequently during the years that followed. Frederik VII himself had approximately sixty order badges among which he could choose, and these miniature order badges made it possible for him to display twenty-six of them without covering his entire jacket. In the picture, a red freemasons' cross is uppermost.

Frederik VII – The Giver of the Constitution

the fortified town of Rendsburg on March 18. These representatives decided to send a deputation to Copenhagen to demand a constitution for Schleswig-Holstein and the incorporation of Schleswig into the German Confederation. During the years that followed, there would be fighting to determine which of three possibilities would prevail: the traditional whole state, an independent Schleswig-Holstein, or an expansion of Denmark to the River Eider (Schleswig's southern border). The nationalist movement desired this third scenario—the incorporation of Schleswig into the Kingdom of Denmark—and this attitude was politically represented by the National Liberals, who called an urgent extraordinary meeting in the Casino Theatre on 20 March. At this meeting, an agitated assembly of 2500 citizens expressed their support for a resolution that rejected the demands made by Schleswig-Holstein and called for a common constitution for Denmark and Schleswig. There was a false rumour to the effect that a revolt had already broken out in the duchies, and this rumour influenced the mood of the people. On the morning of the next day, 21 March, spurred on by the National Liberal, D. G. Monrad, Bardenfleth convinced the King to make the National Liberals' demands his own, and at a meeting of the Council of State that same morning, Fritz gave his ministers a choice between abandoning Christian VIII's whole-state constitution or handing in their resignations. As had been expected, they chose the latter.

Later in the day, the procession of citizens that would later become famous made its way to Christiansborg, where a declaration from the Copenhagen City Council that had been dictated by the National Liberals was read to the King. The declaration demanded the dissolution of the government and ended with a bombastic appeal to His Majesty that he not "drive the nation to take matters in its own hands out of desperation." Frederik VII could inform the citizens that their request had already been fulfilled.

Bardenfleth had to hurry to assembly a new team of ministers, and on the morning of the next day, 22 March, a conservative government had been assembled that was believed to be able to reach a peaceful solution. The same morning, however, Frederik VII received a letter from the Prince of Noer (Frederick of Schleswig-Holstein-Sonderburg-Augustenburg, the governor of the duchies), who threatened to lead an uprising. The King became enraged, and because of this the National Liberals D. G. Monrad, L. N. Hvidt, and Orla Lehmann, were invited to join the government that later became known as the March Ministry.

Frederik VII in an admiral's uniform, painted by H. A. G. Schiött in about 1850. The portrait gives one a sense of the deep insecurity that characterized the King and his reign despite the fact that he was able to get any assembly of people on his side with his simple words and powerful voice.

In the afternoon, when Frederik VII received his new ministers, he declared that he now viewed himself as a constitutional monarch and intended only to participate in meetings of the Council of State when he was called upon to do so. No doubt he said this with a good deal of relief. Formally, the absolute monarchy would continue to exist until 5 June 1849, but Frederik VII had now passed on responsibility for governing Denmark, and later in the day, he could let himself be hailed by thousands of Copenhageners who had assembled on Christiansborg Slotsplads.

# The First Schleswig War

By forcing his ministers to resign, Frederik VII triggered the First Schleswig War. From the moment they came to power, the National Liberals tried desperately to stop the revolt that had made it possible for them to take over in Denmark, but events took their inevitable course. On 23 March, after people in Schleswig-Holstein had read about the casino meeting and the dissolution of the government, it was decided that a provisional government for the duchies would be created. The particular legitimation was the claim that someone would have to govern on behalf of Frederik VII, who was incorrectly said to have acted under duress. On 24 March, the Prince of Noer was able to take the fort at Rendsburg without encountering any resistance—most of the garrison joined the revolt—and with this, war was inevitable. When a deputation from the duchies finally arrived in Copenhagen, its demands were utterly rejected, and it was informed that Holstein was to have its own constitution while Schleswig and the Kingdom of Denmark were to have a common constitution.

At the Battle of Bov on 9 April 1848, the army of Schleswig-Holstein suffered a defeat, and many of its soldiers were taken prisoner. The Danish army advanced south to the Danevirke, but the revolutionary government received support from Prussia, which changed the balance of power. In the Battle of Schleswig on 23 April, the Danes were forced to retreat, after which the Prussian army occupied Northern Schleswig (except Als and Ærø) as well as large parts of Jutland. Luckily for Denmark, the Czar of Russia pressured the King of Prussia to pull out of the war, and the German troops began to withdraw in late May.

A ceasefire lasting seven months was negotiated, but it did not prove to be possible to secure the peace in the course of these months. In Copenhagen, even the National Liberal ministers were in fact now prepared to divide Schleswig in accordance with the results of a referendum—as ultimately occurred in 1920—but there was strong resistance to such a solution both in Denmark and in the duchies, and the King rendered it completely impossible. This occurred at a royal review of troops in Vejle for which a song had been written in honour of the King. This song ended with the declaration that no one "wants to see our beautiful fatherland divided—this will not happen," and Frederik VII then rose, deeply moved, and loudly declared, "This will not happen—I promise!"

Frederik VII takes leave of his soldiers on Rosenborg Drill Ground in April 1848. This is said to have been a deeply emotional occasion on which Fritz ended by exclaiming, "I'll see you over there!" While formally the King was not the commander-in-chief of the armed forces, Fritz had a habit of speaking as if he were during the First Schleswig War. Drawing by P. C. Klæstrup.

England issued an invitation to a peace conference at which a division of Schleswig could be discussed, but Frederik VII did not feel that he could break his royal promise, and this caused the March Ministry to resign. This was, in fact, the most comfortable solution for the National Liberals, for the division of Schleswig would have made them very unpopular. Frederik VII, having let himself be swept away by popular opinion, thus had a heavy portion of the responsibility for the continued fighting over Schleswig.

In April 1849, the fighting resumed with renewed intensity. Schleswig-Holstein's army of twenty thousand men was still supported by the German Confederation, which provided a further forty thousand soldiers; Denmark could field forty-one thousand. The German troops again advanced into Jutland while the army of Schleswig-Holstein besieged Fredericia. It proved to be possible to send new troops to support the city, and on 6 July, the Danes executed a successful breakout attack. Almost at the same time in Berlin, agreement was reached regarding a provisional peace agreement according to which Schleswig would get its own constitution, but there was such great resistance on both sides that further negotiations the following year failed to produce a result. In July 1850, Denmark and Prussia concluded a simple peace agreement that made no provision for an ultimate solution, but the following month in London, the non-German great powers and the Nordic countries reached agreement regarding a protocol securing the indivisibility and integrity of the Danish monarchy. This meant that the old whole state was to be reestablished.

Schleswig-Holstein resumed fighting the war on its own, and on July 25, the war's bloodiest battle was fought at Isted. A force of 36.500 Danish soldiers engaged Schleswig-Holstein's army of 26,800, which resulted in approximately 1,400 dead, many more wounded, and the withdrawal of Schleswig-Holstein's troops. The government and army of Schleswig-Holstein were finally dissolved in January 1851, after which Prussia and Austria occupied Holstein while Denmark secured control of Schleswig down to the River Eider. Prussia did not recognize the London protocol, but Denmark succeeded in concluding the so-called Agreements of 1851–1852 with the German powers. A main point of these agreements was that Schleswig was not to be integrated with Denmark or Holstein, and the subsequently agreed-upon January proclamation foresaw a common constitution for Denmark and the duchies as a supplement to the Kingdom's constitution.

The question of the order of succession in Schleswig and Holstein still required a solution, however, not least because an important premise in connection with the First Schleswig War had been that the House of Augustenburg could lay claim to a right of inheritance in the duchies if the Oldenburg line of monarchs died out. With the London treaty of 8 Ma 1852, the European powers therefore recognized Prince Christian of Glücksburg as possessing the hereditary right to succeed to the Danish throne, which had been possible because his wife, Princess Louise, possessed the right of inheritance and could transfer this right to her husband. Prince Christian was a proponent of the whole-state solution and therefore qualified to guarantee compliance with the peace treaty despite the fact that his brothers had fought on the side of Schleswig-Holstein. This new order of succession was the most tangible result of the First Schleswig War,

By staying close to the spring fighting, the King made himself extremely popular among the Danish troops. Here he is shown at the fateful review of troops at Lerbæk Field. After the parade, the King promised that Schleswig would not be divided. Drawing by P.C. Klæstrup.

*Previous spread:*
Constantin Hansen's
five-metre-
wide painting of
the Constituting
National Assembly's
opening meeting on
23 October 1848.
It was painted
during the period
1860–64. In the
foreground are the
National Liberals;
the painting
represents the
King's perspective.
In the chamber at
Christiansborg at
that time, the King's
throne stood at
the position from
which one sees
the assembly in
the picture. At the
vanishing point of
this perspective,
one can see the
poet and priest N.
F. S. Grundtvig,
which is the artist's
subtle way of saying
that democracy
should be based on
a Grundtvigian view
of life.

which generally resulted in a confirmation of the status quo. In Denmark, however, the war was interpreted as having ended with a glorious Danish victory, and for the rest of his reign, the king could ride on a wave of popularity that had been created by the war.

Fritz greatly enjoyed telling stories of how bullets had whistled around his ears during his inspections of the Danish positions. When he had visited Flensburg, a shot had been heard that in his tireless imagination was transformed into an assassination attempt in which the bullet had cut the reins of his horse. And he could now attribute his old hand injury to the Battle of Isted despite the fact that Fritz had actually been fishing in Northern Zealand when the battle took place.

## The June Constitution

In 1848, the advisory assemblies of the estates of the realm were called together in Roskilde and Viborg for the last time to approve election legislation so that elections to the Constituting National Assembly could be held. All men of good reputation over thirty years of age who were heads of their own households were to have the right to vote in the election. There was a fair amount of friction due to the fact that the government had appointed thirty-eight representatives chosen by the King to the assembly who would join 114 representatives elected by the people. The National Assembly carried out its work on the basis of a draft constitution prepared by D. G. Monrad and Orla Lehmann, and the extent of suffrage became the most important point of contention during the composition of the first Danish constitution. It proved possible to agree on a compromise featuring general suffrage in connection with elections to a parliament with two chambers, such that men over thirty with their own households could vote in elections to the Folketing, while elections to the Landsting would be indirect and the right to vote in those elections would be restricted to well-to-do men over forty. Approximately fifteen percent of the population got the right to vote, which was extraordinarily democratic by the standards of the time.

The Constitutional Act of the Kingdom of Denmark was adopted by a solid majority and signed by Frederik VII on 5 June 1849. The constitution began with a reservation to the effect that Schleswig's situation would have to remain unresolved until the war had ended, but the constitution never went into effect

Photograph of Countess Danner. Fritz is said to have taken this picture with him everywhere and placed it on his desks in the various places where he stayed.

It is believed that this gold ring inset with diamonds was a gift from the King to Countess Danner. The inscription "Frederik VII" goes all the way around the ring.

south of the Kongeå. Also, the original constitution's specifications with regard to suffrage did not remain in effect long, despite the fact that the prospect of broad suffrage had helped mobilize the Danes during the war. Suffrage was progressively restricted several times—in the Common Constitution of 1855, in the

Frederik VII's trademark red fez, which he wore at home and on informal occasions. He was amused by dressing provocatively; it was almost as if he were acting in a play. A well-known anecdote has it that Frederik VII once said to an actor, "Actually, we are colleagues! The only difference between us is that you only have to act in a comedy in the evening, while I sometimes have to do so all day long!"

November Constitution of 1863, and, in particular, in the revised Constitution of 1866. Nevertheless, the June Constitution represented the formal basis of democracy in Denmark, and much of it was transmitted word for word into the revised constitutions of 1915 and 1953.

## Countess Danner

Fritz is said to have made a solemn promise to his dying father that "the woman" would never enter the palace, but only a week after Frederik VII's accession to the throne, Louise moved in at Christiansborg and was thereafter to be addressed as Madame Danner. Carl Berling, too, noticed that his friend had become King, for immediately after Frederik VII's accession, he was appointed the King's private secretary, and later, he also became the general treasurer of the court. The trio were together again, but now, they spent their time in rooms with higher ceilings.

In March 1848, when the transformation of the state had been completed, the King announced to his newly formed government that he intended to marry. After he had given up absolute power, the King felt that he had the right to arrange his private life as he saw fit, but he nevertheless let himself be persuaded to let the potential international scandal wait until after the war. To begin with, he elevated Louise to the nobility as the Baroness of Dannefeldt, having managed to secure the retention of the King's right to grant titles and membership in royal orders. But after the peace agreement had been concluded in Berlin and the London protocol—in which the great powers promised to help find a solution to the problem of the hereditary order of succession—had been signed on 2 August 1850, Fritz did not want to wait any longer. On 7 August, the forty-two-year-old king married the thirty-five-year-old former dancer and illegitimate daughter of a servant girl and her employer. The wedding took place in Frederiksborg Palace Church and was witnessed by some conscripted officials and, as the only royal witness, Hereditary Prince Ferdinand. This was a morganatic marriage, for it was out of the question that Louise could become Queen

Frederik VII engrossed in archaeological studies in his study at Jægerspris Palace, which eventually became the primary residence of the high couple. Against the wall, one can see the King's pipe rack, which contains no fewer than eighty-five pipes. The pipe rack can still be seen in this room today. Drawing by P. C. Klæstrup.

Frederik VII
launched the
excavations of the
old royal graves
in Sorø Church
and Saint Bendt's
Church in Ringsted.
This drawing by P.
C. Klæstrup depicts
the King during the
excavation in 1855.

and give birth to heirs to the throne. However, she could now call herself the Countess of Danner.

The wedding was not publicized, for Fritz knew very well that his marriage would cause problems. It was simply outside the limits of imaginable social mobility that a king would marry an illegitimate child of the working class, and it was also quite significant that he had thus permanently blocked any possibility of producing a legitimate heir. Fritz and Louise were nevertheless shocked by the number of humiliations and insults they, in fact, faced after the news had become publicly known. Foreign diplomats were instructed to ignore the Countess, and in Copenhagen high society, she was boycotted outright. The marriage could in no way be accepted by the other members of the Royal Family, and it was opposed both by the aristocracy and by the National Liberal academic bourgeoisie that set the tone in the 1850s. There was thus a permanent conflict between the pair and representatives of their closest social and political environment, and as a result, they ended up spending most of their time outside the capital—at the palaces at Jægerspris and Frederiksborg as well as in Skodsborg, where the King bought a country estate in Strandvejen.

The marriage was not rendered less controversial by Louise's political activism. In addition to Højre (the Conservatives) and the National Liberals, the political landscape of the early Danish democracy also featured the Society of Farmers' Friends, which drew its support mostly from the rural population. They found a natural ally in the Countess, Carl Berling having acted as the contact person, and it was after having been encouraged to do so by the Farmers' Friends that Louise began her charity work, which eventually became quite extensive. It was also with their encouragement that, in 1851, she and Fritz began to travel around the kingdom together. First, they tried undertaking a trip to Bornholm, where the local officials received them politely while their wives remained at home—the way this was done in Copenhagen. Nevertheless, the inhabitants of Bornholm proved to be much more accommodating in their encounters with the high couple than the people they were used to meeting, and Fritz and Louise had similar experiences during a series of visits to provincial Denmark they undertook during the years that followed.

The trips contributed to making Louise a more public figure, and this was necessary. In fact, Louise was really a kind of mother to Fritz, who was highly de-

Frederik VII's general's helmet. The helmet was made by J. B. Dalhoff in about 1859 in aluminium, a newly discovered, lightweight, and very expensive metal.

pendent on having her in his vicinity. She was able to calm him so that he did not scandalize people with his drinking, his hot temperament, and his much too lively imagination. For this reason, the Countess was always nearby when Fred-

Frederik VII was especially fond of uniforms, and he had some highly original ones made. The picture shows his general's uniform with scarf, rapier, harness, cartridge bag, and order badges. With this uniform, the king wore his aluminium helmet.

erik VII was giving an audience or otherwise appearing in public, and she had to accept the fact that people despised her.

## The Danish nationalist king of the whole state

The international agreements meant that after the war, a constitution for the whole state was to be drafted, and Frederik VII played a key role in efforts to do so. The project was difficult to complete, particularly because the duchies had returned to the old system in which the King was theoretically an absolute monarch advised by assemblies of the estates of the realm.

In 1854, a conservative government led by A. S. Ørsted finished work on a draft of a constitution for the Kingdom and the duchies that would mean a significant strengthening of the political power of the monarchy in relation respectively to the parliament and the assemblies of the estates of the realm in the duchies. Not surprisingly, this draft encountered resistance, so the King scheduled elections. After the government had suffered a dramatic defeat, a new government was formed consisting of supporters of the whole-state solution as well as moderate National Liberals, and in October 1855, this government was able to secure a majority for a common constitution. This new constitution restricted the June Constitution's area of validity to the Kingdom's special affairs and represented a significant step backward for Danish democracy. Worse yet, the constitution did not lead to the intended calming of the disputes regarding the whole state. Holstein continued to insist on the same constitutional conditions for itself as those that would apply to Denmark, and because of this, the constitution's applicability to Holstein had to be nullified three years later.

During his entire reign, Frederik VII faced the general dilemma that he had inherited the whole state from his father and felt that he had a duty to uphold his father's legacy, but at the same time viewed the problem of Schleswig with Danish nationalist eyes. "His heart was Danish," as people so beautifully put it, and while he found himself in an oppositional relationship with the National Liberals because of their hostility to the Countess, he did share their view that all of Schleswig was—or should be—Danish. Indeed, he could easily accept the implementation of a policy of active Danification in Schleswig after the area had been won back, a policy that contributed to perpetuating a German notion that Denmark was an enemy.

Carl Berling, painted by the artist Edward Young, who was at the court for some years and was rumoured to be Countess Danner's lover. Berling himself was also rumoured to be the Countess's lover, even after Fritz and Louise had been married. However, the most apparently significant testimony regarding both of these extramarital relationships came from people at the court who were openly hostile to Berling and the Countess.

It was a constant problem that because of his marriage, Fritz lacked competent advisors. He had to rely on friends he personally trusted, and the most important criterion was that they recognized Louise's status as his wife. However, he did find an influential political partner in L. N. Scheele, a Holstein official who had been a favourite of Christian VIII and whom Frederik VII called upon in 1854 to resolve the dispute over the constitution proposed by the Ørsted government.

Frederiksborg
Palace on fire.
Painted by
Ferdinand Rickardt
in 1859.

Countess Danner in the company of the Egyptian prince, Muhammad Ali. When there was to be a formal dinner at Christiansborg on the occasion of the prince's visit, the National Liberal minister of the interior A. F. Krieger demonstrated his opposition to the Countess by threatening to resign if she came to the table together with the King. The compromise arrived at was that she was brought to the table by Hereditary Prince Ferdinand, so it must be assumed that this 1859 sketch by Wilhelm Marstrand shows a different situation during the prince's visit. It was claimed that Muhammad Ali was three times as fat as the King, which would have made the prince quite large.

During the following years, Scheele was a key political figure due to the fact that he stood in the King's favour, but he, too, eventually had everyone against him because of his support for the Countess. In 1857, he had to give up trying to form a government and returned to Holstein, after which Carl Berling was the King's only loyal friend who had a significant number of useful contacts.

## The fire

In 1858 and 1859, just when the King and the Countess were most isolated, there was an unexpected turn of events. The National Liberals, who were led by A. F. Krieger, had long wished to have Berling removed from the court, both because of moral indignation over his relationship with Louise and because of the role he played as a liaison between the king and the Farmers' Friends. On several occasions, Berling had acted carelessly—for example, he had accused prominent Swedes of being behind some of the many published attacks on the Countess—and this caused the government, which was now led by C. C. Hall, to present an ultimatum regarding Berling's dismissal.

When Frederik VII refused to agree to Berling's removal, the National Liberal ministers resigned in the belief that as before, the King would take them back because he lacked a better option, but now, the King surprisingly succeeded in forming an alternative government led by C. E. Rotwitt with support from the Farmers' Friends. This government was directly opposed to the National Liber-

Frederik VII painted by Johan Vilhelm Gertner in 1861.

Theatre binoculars with Countess Danner's crowned monogram and coat of arms as well as miniatures of Frederiksberg Palace and Fredensborg Palace. A present from the Swedish king, Charles XV, in commemoration of Charles XV's visit to Denmark in 1862.

als, and its critics called it the Countess's special ministry. The ministers were public servants, not prominent politicians, and several of them were close acquaintances of the high couple.

The government had to function in the National Liberal bastion of Copenhagen, where the media were boiling with rage. One week after the formation of the government, Copenhagen experienced the premiere of a play called The Countess and Her Sibling's Child that was full of malicious references, and while the citizens of the capital city were thus entertained, Fritz and Louise went to stay at Frederiksborg as they had so often done before. In the early hours of 17 Decem-

ber 1859, during this stay, the palace burned down, probably because of a newly installed fireplace in the attic room containing the King's collection of antiquities. The loss of a collection of archaeological finds that had grown to include six thousand items was a personal disaster for the King, but far worse was the loss of a huge number of irreplaceable paintings and other art objects and interiors. However, Fritz reacted calmly, having understood that the fire had gotten out of control. All he asked to have saved was a photograph of his mother's grave in Rome.

The destruction of Christian IV's magnificent palace was a national catastrophe, and newspapers and magazines associated the fire with the resistance to the Countess, interpreting the destruction of the palace as divine justice. During the

Shortly before his death, Frederik VII became very worried when he visited the Danevirke fortifications. After the outbreak of war the following year, the fortifications had to be evacuated because a hard frost had made it possible for the enemy to cross the wetlands.

FOLKETS KIÆRLIGHED

MIN STYRKE

days around Christmas, flyers were handed out demanding that the Countess and Berling should be removed from the court, and around the beginning of the new year, there were demonstrations and even riots. Berling had fallen during the fire and suffered a serious back injury that in fact forced him to give up his public offices, but this did not result in a significantly improved public mood. The unrest reduced the authority of the government, and when Rotwitt suddenly died on 6 February 1860, no one wanted to take over. This meant the end of the Countess's ministry and the advent of a new National Liberal government that revived the demand that Denmark's southern border be moved down to the Eider during the years that followed.

The death medal of the Order of Freemasons for Frederik VII. The inscription on the back reads, "May promises fulfilled comfort him in death."

## November 1863

The last years of Frederik VII's reign were characterized by a certain resignation. Fritz and Louise withdrew to Jægerspris Palace, ownership of which he had transferred to her, and toward the end of the King's life, even she was unable to control his drinking. His health began to fail, and during a trip to Schleswig in the fall of 1863, he contracted rosacea (a skin infection), which is not normally fatal but appears to have been the primary cause of Frederik VII's death at Glücksburg Palace on 15 November.

Two days before the King's death, the November Constitution—a common constitution for the Kingdom and Schleswig—had been adopted despite bitter pro-

The equestrian statue of Frederik VII on Christiansborg Slotsplads by H. W. Bissen was financed by means of collection of funds in the capital and was unveiled in 1873. It says much about the hatred people felt toward Countess Danner that ten years after Frederik VII's death she was not welcome at the unveiling of the statue, which she watched from a palace window.

tests from the German Confederation. This constitution violated the Agreements of 1851–1852, and Prussia made it fairly clear that its adoption could lead to war. However, public support for the new constitution was overwhelming, in part because it was hoped that a Scandinavian military alliance would be formed. The friendship between Frederik VII and the Swedish king, Charles XV, contributed to this hope, and during an informal visit to Skodsborg, the Swedish king had actually promised Swedish aid if there were a war—even though Charles XV had lacked a mandate from his government for the issuance of such a promise.

The new king, Christian IX, had originally been chosen as a successor to the throne because he was considered a suitable candidate for maintaining the whole-state model, but he was now forced to sign a constitution to which he was strongly opposed. The result was the complete loss of the duchies of Schleswig, Holstein, and Lauenburg in a bloody war the following year.

## The legacy

It is worth thinking about how Frederik VII might have been remembered if he had lived a year longer. The Danish defeat in 1864 was the consequence of a political attitude that had been supported by the King, and if he had lived through the war, his reign would have appeared in a different and tragic light. Even in death, this remarkable king proved to have been a master of timing. His accession to the throne in 1848, the year of revolutions, had granted him the historical privilege of taking on the role of the giver of the June Constitution, and when, by passing away, he left it to Christian IX to sign the November Constitution, it was almost as if Fritz had seen an opportunity to escape his responsibility one last time.

For many years thereafter, Frederik VII represented one of two notions of what a constitution should be. The revised Constitution of 1866 gave real control of the Landsting to the aristocracy and the major landowners, who held power during almost the entirety of Christian IX's reign. Because of this, Frederik VII remained a relevant figure as the king who had transferred his power to the people by means of the June Constitution—the most democratic constitution that had yet been seen in Denmark—while Christian IX was hailed by Højre and its supporters because he had introduced the Constitution of 1866. Thanks to supporters of

As the sole heir to the king's private fortune, Countess Danner was able to launch some major charity projects. She had this building in Nansensgade built for her foundation for retired working-class women, which was established in 1873. In 1979, the foundation was dissolved and the house sold, but representatives of the women's movement occupied the house in November of the same year and ultimately bought it following the great Countess Danner fund-raising drive. Since then, the Danner House has been a crisis centre and asylum for women who have been victims of violence.

reform, no fewer than forty-six monuments to Christian IX's predecessor were erected during Christian's own reign.

Despite Frederik VII's obvious weaknesses, his scandalous marriages, and his large share of the responsibility for the wars over Schleswig, the June Constitution ended up trumping everything else, for which people were happy to forgive him. More than anything else, his reciprocated love for the people coloured his legacy, and in fact, Frederik VII can be seen as playing a key role in the self-understanding of the Danes. The Danes' view of themselves as peace-loving people who are able to solve problems through calm discussion can be traced directly back to the events of 1848. It can be seen as paradoxical because the Danish March revolution triggered a civil war, but Frederik VII did pave the way for the transformation of the international freedom movement into a constructive constitutional project that would lead to the termination of the absolute monarchy. For this reason, it is basically justified to call him the giver of the Constitution.

# SUGGESTIONS FOR
# FURTHER READING

Jan Møller, *Frederik 7—En kongeskæbne,* Forlaget Sesam, 1994.
An easy-to-read biography.

Birgitte Nyborg, *Charlotte Frederikke, Frederik VII's mor—En historisk biografi,*
Forlaget Falcon, 2015.
A thorough biography of one of the forgotten and unusual figures of Danish
history based on contemporary sources.

Hans Vammen, *Den Tomme Stat—Angst og ansvar i dansk politik 1848–1864,*
Museum Tusculanums Forlag, 2011.
An in-depth analysis of the shifting political landscape under Frederik VII
featuring detailed portraits of the leading politicians of the age.

Claus Bjørn, *1848—Borgerkrig og revolution,* Gyldendal, 1998.
A good book about the most important year in the life of Frederik VII.

Birger Mikkelsen, *Konge til Danmark—En biografi af Frederik VII,* Nordisk Forlag
for Videnskab og Teknik, 1982.
The most detailed biography of Frederik VII yet written. The book does not
contain actual references to sources, but it is rich in information.

kongernessamling.dk

**Frederik VII**
The Giver of the Constitution

Copyright © 2017
The Royal Danish Collection and Historika / Gads Forlag A/S

ISBN: 978-87-93229-79-2
First edition, first print run

Printed in Lithuania

Text: Jens Gunni Busck
Edited by Birgit Jenvold
Translated from Danish by Peter Sean Woltemade
Cover and graphic design Lene Nørgaard, Le Bureau
Printed by Clemenstrykkeriet, Lithuania

Illustrations:
P. 36-37, 48-49: The Museum of National History, Frederiksborg Castle
(photo: Kit Weiss), p. 50: National Gallery of Denmark; all other illustrations: The Royal Danish Collection.